Mountainside Prayer

Mountainside Prayer

Words and Deeds That Rise

THOMAS NISBETT

RESOURCE *Publications* • Eugene, Oregon

MOUNTAINSIDE PRAYER
Words and Deeds That Rise

Copyright © 2026 Thomas Nisbett. All rights reserved. Except for brief quotations in critical publications or reviews, no part of this book may be reproduced in any manner without prior written permission from the publisher. Write: Permissions, Wipf and Stock Publishers, 199 W. 8th Ave., Suite 3, Eugene, OR 97401.

Resource Publications
An Imprint of Wipf and Stock Publishers
199 W. 8th Ave., Suite 3
Eugene, OR 97401

www.wipfandstock.com

PAPERBACK ISBN: 979-8-3852-7559-5
HARDCOVER ISBN: 979-8-3852-7560-1
EBOOK ISBN: 979-8-3852-7561-8

VERSION NUMBER 03/13/26

Scripture quotations marked (NASB) are taken from the (NASB®) New American Standard Bible®, Copyright © 1960, 1971, 1977, 1995, 2020 by The Lockman Foundation. Used by permission. All rights reserved. www.lockman.org

Scripture quotations marked MSG are taken from The Message, copyright © 1993, 2002, 2018 by Eugene H. Peterson. Used by permission of NavPress, represented by Tyndale House Publishers, Inc. All rights reserved.

Scripture quotations marked (NLT) are taken from the Holy Bible, New Living Translation, copyright ©1996, 2004, 2015 by Tyndale House Foundation. Used by permission of Tyndale House Publishers, Carol Stream, Illinois 60188. All rights reserved.

Scripture quotations marked (ESV) are taken from The ESV® Bible (The Holy Bible, English Standard Version®), copyright © 2001 by Crossway, a publishing ministry of Good News Publishers. Used by permission. All rights reserved.

Scripture quotations marked (NIV) are taken from the Holy Bible, New International Version®, NIV®. Copyright © 1973, 1978, 1984, 2011 by Biblica, Inc.™ Used by permission of Zondervan. All rights reserved worldwide. www.zondervan.com The "NIV" and "New International Version" are trademarks registered in the United States Patent and Trademark Office by Biblica, Inc.™

Bible text from the Good News Translation (GNT) is not to be reproduced in copies or otherwise by any means except as permitted in writing by American Bible Society, 101 North Independence Mall East, FL 8, Philadelphia, PA 19106 -2155 (www.americanbible.org).

I don't think it is enough appreciated how much an outdoor book the Bible is. It's best read and understood outdoors, and the further outdoors the better.
—Wendell Berry

Contents

THE THIRD STRAND: *PRAYER PRACTICES FOR HEARING GOD*

THE FOURTH STRAND: *CLIMBING PRAYER MOUNTAIN*

Acknowledgments

As I recall the names and faces of my prayer mentors—Jordan, Eloise, Joe, Gail, Donna, Roberta, Terry, J. T., Bill, Gordon—they glowed because they lived close to God. It showed on their faces.

My prayer partners are too numerous to mention and, yet they are "a manifold witness to Thy great faithfulness, mercy, and love." They are the communion of saints, now living and those who have died in Christ.

Shall I list all the books on prayer in my personal library, written by my spiritual friends through the ages that have instructed me to pray? I count at least 50 on the shelf in my study. We stand on the shoulders of those who came before us.

Abstract: *What is Mountainside Prayer?*

We live and work and sleep indoors. We've detached ourselves from nature. Some people walk and pray and that's good. How many of us daily retreat alone to a quiet place outside with God? *Jesus did.* A retreat into nature provides a space for spiritual fortification and preparation. The mountain symbolizes a place of God's presence, a place of strength and permanence.

On the side of a mountain as recorded in Matthew's gospel, Jesus gave his disciples the Lord's Prayer, a perfect model for effective praying. He tells them not to pray like the religious leaders do—in the synagogues, on street corners, in temples, and to be seen by other people. His followers have the power of inner withdrawal in the intimacy of heartfelt communion with God.

Going to the mountain to pray reveals a desire to be alone with God. *Like desire produces discipline, prayer produces action.* Here is the sequence: living close to God (listening prayer) generates words and deeds that rise (activated faith) and establishes prayer practices (obeying God). *As Moses went up to meet God, God spoke to him from the mountain.*

There are seven accounts from the Gospels indicating that Jesus practiced mountainside prayer to connect with God. Seven prayer-soaked stories from practical missions inspire us to allow our words and deeds to rise. These actions provide spiritual *strength* and *stretch*. Ten approaches from the mountain will be your *sheath* through abrasive times and harsh resistance on your prayer journey of obeying God.

STARTING WELL

I have decided to follow Jesus,
no turning back, no turning back.

If you have committed yourself to Jesus Christ, to be a climbing companion of His, you will no doubt hike the hills and valleys of life following in His footsteps. You will find the terrain uneven and steep, ascending and descending. The mountainside will be your place of prayer, more than the closet. At times and through the seasons of living, the surface beneath your feet will be steep *and* icy. You will be glad that you are *roped* to Him. *He holds all Creation together. Col. 1:17 (NLT)*

There are three strands, perhaps four, in this climbing rope of prayer that we are weaving, a lifeline to God in a lifetime of listening. Strong dynamic climbing ropes are constructed from nylon which has *strength and stretch* properties. The nylon material is made into tiny fibers that are spun into threads which are then woven together as strands: *strength and stretch* for core material, abrasion resistance and durability with the *sheath* material. We will consider a fourth strand after Section Three.

Our climbing rope of prayer is no Jacob's Ladder nor Stairway to Heaven. *If you see a young disciple, by his own will climbing up into heaven, one elder said, take him by the foot and throw him to the ground, because what he is doing is not good for him. (Desert Fathers)* Raw human effort is not dependence on God.

Like Jacob's Ladder, the climbing rope *is* a metaphor for God's promise to be present with us and keep us wherever we go, tethered to him. Missionary E. Stanley Jones exhorted Christ followers to "Work like it was all up to you *and* trust like it was all up to God." Begin your prayer time with this statement: *Today, I will not struggle and try, I will surrender and trust.*

What are the three strands of this prayer rope? First, the strand of living close to God—regularly, routinely, repeatedly. That is the *core strength.* Second, the strand of words and deeds that rise as a memorial to God, the practice of sacrificing time and money. That is the *core stretch.* Third, the prayer practices for obeying God, the *sheath* which produces durability in abrasive times. *A rope made of three strands of cord is hard to break.*

Rope Up! Jesus is on lead.

THE FIRST STRAND

Living Close to God

A Lonely Place

"In the early morning, while it was still dark, Jesus got up, left the house, and went to a secluded place, and was praying there."
—Mark 1:35 (NASB)

Some translations of Mark record the words "long before dawn." Do you get up to pray long before dawn? Or are you an early riser, a morning person who squeezes in a quick devotional reading while waiting for your coffee? Maybe you will sleep in. Not Jesus. Here in Mark's concise gospel account is the first indication of what, in his life, was a great priority of Jesus: the renewal of life in prayer.

David McKenna writes, "Temptation continues to buffet Jesus from many sides. After a successful day in which he casts out demons and heals the sick, he runs the risk of exhausting his energies and losing his perspective. Jesus needs solitude. So, long before daylight on the morning after his day of success, he goes alone and prays."[1]

Here in the lonely place is the secret of renewal, the private solitude in the secluded place of prayer. Jesus didn't take time out for prayer. It was time into him for the re-creation of life and the fresh realignment to the will of his Father. *You need this.* You need

1. David McKenna, *Mark: The Communicator's Commentary*. Waco, TX: Word Books, 1979, page 53.

these three strands of the rope that are hard to break: freedom, fulfillment, and the fact of prayer, provided in the lonely place.

First, this lonely place was not a passive posture for Jesus. He was as active here privately as he was publicly healing the people who crowded about him. Prayer is the highest activity of mind and spirit. True activity is never rightly measured by noise or motion. For Jesus the secret of sustained life and inner strength was the opening of his soul to the unseen realm—God's Kingdom. It is for his followers the *freedom* of the sustained life of the Spirit in us.

Second, there can be no *fulfillment* without a lonely place. Lacking it, life lacks the dimension of height. And that is precisely the case in so many people's lives. The physical conditions of existence seem often enough to make solitude impossible. "I don't have the time or the place," say modern city dwellers. It is hard to shut out the insistent intrusions of the outer world. Lift your inner world.

Third, we must *make* a lonely place. Nothing that enriches and empowers life ever just "happens." It is made. That is a *fact.* Jesus never "happened" to find himself alone in prayer. He went out to put a strong hedge around some corner of time and space. The busy life which never does that has no means of renewal, of cleansing, of fortification. Private prayer is beautifully pictured in Keat's line: "I stood tiptoe on a little hill." Jesus did it in Galilee. *You can do it on your hill*!

A Desolate Place

"But Jesus himself would often slip away to the wilderness and pray."
—Luke 5:16 (NASB)

Jesus had just cleansed a man of leprosy and the news about him was spreading, creating crowds who want to hear him and be healed. The Son of God set the example for his followers' prayer lives. Follow Me, follow my example. If Jesus needed to get away and pray to face life, *how much more do we?*

For Jesus that regularly meant going to a place away from people—to a desolate place, to the desert, to the wilderness, to the mountainside. Where is your quiet mountainside? *But . . . I'm too busy . . . I live in a large city . . . I just can't make time in nature . . . I'm afraid of being alone outside.*

Jesus would withdraw to a desolate place. "Desolate" is an important word choice. It can mean a bleak, depressing, or dry place, like the desert. It is the opposite of fertile and populous. It is a place deserted of people and in a state of quiet emptiness. The wild and desolate place contains no human distractions, allowing one to be alone with God. Hike up the hillside in the dark. Go to the park when it's empty. Sit down with God in your backyard.

As often as possible Jesus withdrew to out-of-the-way places for prayer. People continue in our time to want a quick fix for their bodily ailments, a miracle. Refusing the daily practice of living close to God, we live empty lives passed down to us from our forefathers. Jesus needed to be prayer-full to heal not only bodies but also infirmities of the soul. That is deep work. It requires a source of power beyond mere human strength and effort.

Perhaps Jesus retreated to practice intercessory prayer, praying hard for those neighbors or crowds with whom he was not in direct contact. Do we go off somewhere in silent communion with God, interceding for the one with deep needs? This kind of intercession may be the channel through which alone the prevailing help of God comes down.

My friend Bob Utley outlines the work of intercessory prayer to which the followers of Christ are called:

A. Prayer is putting into tangible action our belief in a personal, caring God who is present, willing, and able to act on our behalf and others, through our prayers.

B. God has personally limited Himself to act on the prayers of His children in many areas.

C. The major purpose of prayer, our petitions and intercessions, is our fellowship and time with the Triune God.[2]

Where is your desolate place of prayer? What words and deeds rise, do you think, to God from your mountainside time alone?

2. Bob Utley, FreeBibleCommentary.com. Marshall, TX: Bible Lessons International, 2025.

A High Place

"Six days later Jesus took with him Peter and James and John his brother and led them up a high mountain by themselves."
—Matthew 17:1 (NASB)

We learn in the parallel account from Luke 9:28 that this "metamorphosis" occurred while they were praying on a high mountain. Jesus often prayed alone on a mountainside but on this occasion, he took three climbing companions with him, always teaching them Kingdom truths. It may have been at night after a long hike up the mountain, the mountain of transfiguration, high up and close to God.

The theological connotation is that Jesus' eternal divine nature broke through his human nature. "Sunlight poured from His face. His clothes were filled with light." The very Spirit of God was moving across his humanness, revealing whom he really was. "In the beauty of the lilies Christ was born across the sea with a beauty in his bosom that transfigures you and me." The hope of the True Light!

Christ followers who are serious about their faith devote time daily to prayer. These three disciples made up an inner circle, not of Jesus' favorites, but of those who possibly were more spiritually attuned and teachable. Jesus climbed a mountain, and his true climbing companions followed Him up.

This experience might be called "a glimpse of the Kingdom." We recall Jesus' words in the Lord's Prayer: "Thy Kingdom come; thy will be done on earth as it is in heaven." On the mountain a voice came from the cloud with the supreme statement: "This is My beloved Son, in whom I am well-pleased. Listen to Him." Every morning prayer time may include more silence than voices from heaven. Be expectant. Listen for the holy whisper of God.

The practice of regular prayer is transformational, life changing. Be transformed into a higher nature. "Become partakers of the divine nature." (2 Peter 1:4) You are growing closer to God. You are becoming, by prayer, a friend of God. Jesus said to his disciples, "I no longer call you servants, but I call you friends." (John 15:15 ESV)

You did not choose Me, but I chose you, revealing a daily humility reminder to His first disciples and to current followers. "At the bottom of the mountain, they were met by a crowd of waiting people. What a faithless generation! No sense of God! No focus to your lives!" (Matthew 17:17 MSG)

Don't look for shortcuts to God. The marketplace is flooded with surefire, easygoing formulas for a successful life. Don't fall for that stuff, even though crowds of people do. The way to life—to God—is vigorous and requires total attention! (Matthew 7:13 MSG) *Few find it.*

Jesus chose a mountain. Where do you climb to pray and see the Son rise?

A Mountain Place

"In these days Jesus went out to a mountainside to pray, and all night he continued in prayer to God."
—Luke 6:12 (ESV)

In the Book of Psalms mountains are places of safety, strength, and permanence. Jesus went out to the mountain. It was his habit—regularly, routinely, repeatedly. This retreat followed his healing a man's hand on the Sabbath, resulting in the religious and political leaders being filled with rage and discussing together what they might do to Jesus.

The mountains are also associated with God's descending presence. God comes down so that we can go up. Moses met God on a mountain; Jesus' most memorable teaching was given on a mountainside; three disciples accompanied Jesus on the Mountain of Transfiguration. In this story from Dr. Luke's account, it is uncertain which mountain it is. Whichever high peak he climbed, it was a timely moment to get away and be close to God the Father.

We find in Luke's Gospel narrative more emphases on Jesus' prayer life and his teaching on prayer than any other Gospel writer. Jesus, on this occasion, spent the entire night in prayer before choosing twelve committed companions. Judas the betrayer was one of those powerful choices. He had great potential, and he had a role in the mission. Jesus, full of the Holy Spirit, the Word in the Flesh, still needed to pray over these decisions.

What does your prayer life look like? Have you ever prayed all night over important life decisions as Jesus did? How does one spend the whole night conversing with God? Perhaps by simply being there in his presence, rejoicing, crying, talking, listening. Spending significant time alone with God is the heart of worshipping God.

The power of all-night prayer lies in its ability to help us connect with God more deeply; to get divine intervention in difficult situations or get direction for our life. When we spend an entire night in prayer, we can focus completely on God without the distractions of the day.

In our longer prayer times living closer to God, we are prompted to questions rather than answers. *What is God saying to me? What does God want to do through me? To what person or purpose is God sending me? Whom does God want me to extend forgiveness?* Make space for listening to God.

What is the longest time you've spent in prayer? What did God say to you from His word? Who did God bring to mind?

A Hillside Place

"And Jesus went up on the mountain and sat down there [to pray]."
—Matthew 15: 29–31 (ESV)

On this busy day that followed a walk along the shoreline of the Galilean Sea, Jesus went up the mountain. We humans do find relaxation at the lake or the ocean as we feel the rhythm of the waves and the tidal movement. Our soul seems to align with a natural cycle, not unlike astronomical seasons. We amplify our souls by going up on the mountainside for a larger vision or closer proximity to God.

We do know the context of this verse and the crowds that followed Jesus, indicating that the people could reach him on this hillside or mountainside. They were able to bring the lame, the blind, the mute, the crippled, and many others with them for Jesus to heal. And they glorified the descended God there on the mountain.

Since Jesus *regularly* went up on the mountain to be alone with God, let's linger here a little while. Jesus apparently performed these healings beyond the boundaries of Galilee by ascending into the hills above. Jesus was blessing and healing the stranger as he had blessed his own people. As the first person to ascend the mountainside, Jesus surely wrestled with God over this decision. He had said earlier in his ministry, "I was sent only to the lost sheep of the house of Israel." *Wait*. Does God's redemptive purpose extend to all humans? Pray. Live close to God.

The healings showed even the stranger the weakness of their Gentile gods, and they turned to worship the God of Israel; not, however, the God of Religion, but to the God of Relationships, newly revealed in the compassion of Jesus his son. *Come to Me, all you who are weary and burdened, and I will give you rest.*

Mountainside prayer alone with God, regularly, routinely, repeatedly, reveals God's love for all the world and the desire of God to redeem human nature. *Go to the mountain.* Climb prayer mountain. Get alone with God. Listen.

Track this journey of Jesus from his Sermon on the Mountain to the Healing on the Mountain! Jesus "sat down there," symbolizing an official act of ministry. He shows His power over creation to minister healing and wholeness, compassion on the mountain.

Name your mountainside where you go to be alone with God.

Who has God revealed to you that needs your compassion or forgiveness?

A Regular Place

"After he had dismissed them, he went up on a mountainside by himself to pray."
—Matthew 14:23/ Luke 6: 12–15 (NIV)

Resisting the temptation to be famous, have a title (King), or seek worldly power, Jesus needed to get away, pray, and speak with the Father. The Gospel story repeatedly records Jesus getting alone to pray. If he, being God Incarnate, needed this, how much more do we? Regularly, Routinely, Repeatedly.

Prayer is personal. If you are a person who prays fervently, you pray in your own words. Perhaps you learned how to pray from parents, pastors, or other religious people. Maybe not. Still, as a follower of Jesus, you pray. This is not saying prayers at mealtimes, bedtimes, or good times. *This is listening to God.*

You pray for people and activities close by and for those concerns far away. Sometimes the One to whom you pray seems close and at other times, distant. *Still, you pray.* Prayer is a desire of the human heart. Prayer is also pooled or collective. Deeper prayer is shaped and practiced together with people in whom you have a higher level of trust and connection.

What mountainside prayer represents, in contrast with mountain-moving prayer (Mark 11:23), is habitual prayer, a holy habit. Daily prayer is a consistent practice of one person obeying God, seeking time with God, living close to God. Something so ordinary that anyone can do it, but few choose it—regularly, routinely, repeatedly.

The first disciples of Jesus said to him, "Teach us to pray," implying a depth of relationship with God the Father they did not possess. He said then, "Pray like this."

> *Father, You, Your Name is holy. Your Kingdom is here, and it is coming. Provide what we need daily.* (regularly, routinely, repeatedly) *Forgive us just as we practice forgiveness of everyone, canceling all debts. Lead us not into tempting situations. Deliver us regularly, routinely, repeatedly. So be it.*—Luke 11:14

Name the place you regularly, routinely, and repeatedly go to be alone with God.

Name the person who God has prompted you to forgive.

A Private Place

"My prayer is not for the world, but for those you have given me, because they belong to you."
—John 17: 9 inside verses 1–26.

"Your Father, who sees what is done in secret, will reward you."
—Matthew 6: 6

The focus in Christian faith and practice is the daily discipline of prayer—regularly, routinely, repeatedly—after the example of Jesus. My emphasis in this little book is not on *what* Jesus prayed but on the fact that he did, living close to the Father. However, we have a few stories of what he prayed for in private—his struggle in the Garden of Gethsemane with his fate, "Father, take this cup from me." Or his last prayer as his death on the cross was fulfilled, "Father, forgive them, they do not know what they are doing."

Like the "Lord's Prayer" which Jesus taught his disciples to pray, "The High Priestly Prayer" in John 17, begins with addressing God as Father:

> *These things Jesus spoke; and lifting up His eyes to heaven, He said, 'Father, the hour has come; glorify Thy Son, that the Son may glorify Thee.*

With hands, head, and open eyes lifted toward heaven in a conversation with God, Jesus addressed Deity as "Father." Jesus' Aramaic term was "Abba," which is what a child at home used for his earthly father, "Daddy." This would have been shocking and offensive to the religious non-disciples! I encourage the reader to stop now and read all 26 verses of Jesus' prayer in John 17.

The high priestly prayer falls into three parts: prayer for himself; prayer for his own disciples; and prayer for the unity of the church, the church throughout the centuries. The keynote of every prayer of Jesus is "Father." *For all who are led by the Spirit of God are children of God.* (Romans 8:14)

Believers receive continual guidance from the Spirit, daily prayer, and daily guidance. There is more to Christianity than a decision; it really is an ongoing discipleship. When Jesus prays for himself, he prays, "Learning to know Thee," the only true God. The Son glorifies the Father by completing the work given him to do; the Father will restore the glory partly hidden during the earthly life.

The disciples of Jesus had been given "out of the world" into His care according to God's word, recognizing that Jesus had come from God. Jesus prays for their protection, their unity of heart and mind after the pattern of divine unity, and for the joy to also be theirs. Their mission is to continue the mission of the Son of God.

After praying exclusively for his disciples, Jesus prays for the whole company of the faithful won from the world, for its unity in God, and for the hope born in unity. Jesus prayed for us, his future disciples. When we go outside to pray, we meet with God without distractions: people, phones, or screens. We must live near, and with, and in God. *And we must draw nearer to one another.* The glory of God is mankind alive in this way!

THE SECOND STRAND

Words and Deeds that Rise

A Thoroughly Good Man

---

*"At Caesarea there was a man named Cornelius,
a centurion of what was known as the Italian
cohort, a devout man who feared God with
all his household, gave alms generously to the
people, and prayed continually to God. About
the ninth hour of the day, he saw clearly in a
vision an angel of God come in and say to him,
"Cornelius." And he stared at him in terror and
said, "what is it, Lord?" And he said to him,
"Your prayers and your alms have ascended as
a memorial before God."
—Acts 10:1–4 (ESV)*

Now, read this passage *again* from The Message translation and then we will unpack its meaning:

"There was a man named Cornelius who lived in Caesarea, captain of the Italian guard stationed there. He was a thoroughly good man. He had led everyone in his house to live worshipfully before God, was always helping people in need, and had the habit of prayer. One day at about three o'clock in the afternoon he had a vision. An angel of God, as real as his next-door neighbor, came in and said, 'Cornelius.' Cornelius stared hard, wondering if he was seeing things. Then he said, 'What do you want, sir?' The angel said, 'Your prayers and neighborly acts have brought you to God's attention." *Prayer becomes action.*

Let's explore in reverse order the five Ws as leading questions:

- Who?
- What?
- When?
- Where?
- Why?

Why is this story important? Why does it have a purpose or significance in the larger narrative of the early Christian movement?

Cornelius was a part of an occupying army, and he is described as a God-fearing, devout, good man. This was and still is unusual. He practiced the daily habits of worship, prayer, and giving, teaching his family to do those things as well. The way we treat others and live the Christ-lifestyle will be the standard by which God evaluates our lives.

Where does this story take place?

Caesarea was a seaport on the eastern coast of the Mediterranean between the ancient cities of Dor and Jaffa, originally a small, fortified anchorage named Strabo's Tower. It was the capital of Roman Government in Palestine for over 600 years, serving as the seat of the Roman governors of the province of Judea and headquarters for the Roman legions stationed on the province.

When does this story take place?

The Great Jewish war against Rome began here with an uprising by the Jews in A.D. 66. The Jews were defeated, and Vespasian (A.D. 69–79) was proclaimed emperor by his legions in Caesarea, raising the city to the rank of a Roman colony. According to the Book of Acts which was completed about 62 A.D., Christianity was preached in Caesarea by Philip (8:40) and Peter (10: 1–11), the latter being responsible for the conversion of the Roman Centurion Cornelius.

What objects or actions does this story include?

The acts of worship, generous giving, and daily prayer characterized the life of a Christian, particularly this faithful man and his family. Those actions— the words and the deeds—ascended to God and gained his attention. Your daily prayers and actions "pile-up" and accumulate when you live close to God.

Who is this person? Is he an agent of God's mercy?

Cornelius was his name as you know by now. Its root meaning is "horn" or "little horn" and can be an emblem of power like the Roman river-gods who wore horns. Without a doubt Cornelius was a military man who chose to live righteously before God. He was obedient to God just as his Italian soldiers obeyed his orders.

Another ancient meaning of "horn" was in reference to a mountain peak, an extremity of the earth. The picture of prayers rising from the mountain top or mountain peak fits nicely with the subject of this book—Mountainside Prayers: Words and Deeds that Rise. *The prayers of Cornelius rose to God's attention.*

Serving People in Need

"These twelve disciples Jesus sent out with instructions . . . heal the sick, cleanse the lepers, cast out demons; freely you received, freely give."
—Matthew 10: 5–8 (ESV)

We were in Liberia, West Africa. I was training 60 to 70 pastors in this worn-torn country on topics of daily prayer and spiritual counsel; my brother Rick was continuing his long-term work in public health and education; our medical team of three American doctors were performing fistula repair and VVF surgeries, all of us serving as volunteers. We worked in Monrovia and Ganta.

The first Liberian Civil War was one of two wars in the West African nation of Liberia which lasted between 1989 and 1997. The National Patriotic Front of Liberia (NPFL) led by Charles Taylor took control over most of Liberia within a year, resulting in the deaths of 200,000 civilians. The second war lasted from 1999 to October 2007 with at least 50,000 more deaths. The country was still in shambles and was occupied by 15,000+ armed U. N. Peacekeeping troops when we arrived there in May and June 2008.

My brother had been working in-country for several decades despite the wars. He knew many people and contacts there and made our multiple missions possible. I learned a great deal from him about Liberia's history, its long connection with the U.S., and the recent efforts to re-build damaged infrastructure, institutions, and integrity. I have many stories about "words and deeds that rise." I will share two that impacted me deeply.

The medical surgery team led by Dr. Andy Norman, a mission field doctor who worked in African countries, was amazing. A field hospital is an interesting place. Fistula and VVF surgeons included a young woman doctor from Minnesota with a family back home, and a young male intern from Vanderbilt. The vesicovaginal fistulas (VVF) are usually a tear or hole between the vagina and bladder causing urine leakage, some caused by infection or by obstructed labor during delivery. In Liberia the women may have been raped by soldiers or injured by gun barrels.

Women with this urine leakage were ostracized by their families, rejected from their homes, and shamed. With the news of the visiting doctors at Ganta Hospital, the women needing this surgery lined the hallways and camped on the grounds, awaiting their medical team assessment. Their evaluations began early each day right after the morning chapel and prayers.

I watched Dr. Andy sit beside the women in the halls encouraging them and holding their urine buckets as the catheter drained urine before surgery. He insisted that I hold their buckets as they waited. It was a simple act, and yet, it was more. It honored the women. It was a man respecting a woman who had been shamed. After their successful surgeries, the women were full of joy and smiles filled their faces. The servant acts of doctors, nurses, and volunteers were deeds that rise, humbling to us of course, and hopefully honoring to God.

Following long, humid days of surgeries and pastor training, we needed outside exercise and open vistas. Both the woman doctor and I were regular runners, so we ran the red-dirt roads together for five miles after work. Our talks focused on family and work, my Christian calling to "go into all the world" and her medical vocation to "heal the sick." Despite some church background, she didn't really seem interested in religion.

Our longer runs always took us through the Ganta Leprosy compound founded by Methodist missionary George W. Harley.

Families lived there even if only one family member had this skin condition, and naked children played outside in the trees and dirt fields. My doctor-friend would always stop running, greet and hold the children, and touch the people with leprosy.

I was humbled low just observing. I had always thought that I was following the instructions of Jesus and loving all people, but I hesitated to hold and touch this group. Some of my caution was ignorance of the disease and that's okay. But the woman doctor showed unconditional love and care for strangers. *I had conditions.* She looked more like Jesus than the "Christian." Her words and her deeds were ones that rise, given freely.

The Language of Desperation

"These twelve disciples Jesus sent out with instructions . . . heal the sick, cleanse the lepers, cast out demons; freely you received, freely give."
—Matthew 10: 5–8 (ESV)

We were in Shahdol, Madhya Pradesh, Central India. Our team was training hundreds of pastors in church planting, local church ministry, healing prayer, and understanding scripture. In my sessions I taught from a Eugene Peterson book, *Working the Angles: The Shape of Pastoral Integrity,* focusing on three basic acts—praying, studying scripture, and giving spiritual direction.[3]

Among the hundreds of pastors were a few women pastors and ministers, one woman pastor particularly inspired us. She had been paralyzed from her waist down and crawled on the ground most of her life. She was always nicely attired in dresses and leggings, using her arms to drag her body across the floor, into classrooms, and up and down the stairs. You had to see her to believe it. She attended every session and always smiled, her face radiant with joy. Her name could have been "Joy." She was one of us, teaching us by example—joyful obedience, perseverance of the saints, overcoming present sufferings. Her daily acts of courage, routine perhaps to her, were "deeds that rise."

3. Eugene Peterson, *Working the Angles: The Shape of Pastoral Integrity.* Grand Rapids: Eerdmans, 1989, page 2.

Following our week-long training event, one of the local pastors who travelled all over India encouraging and planting churches, led us far up into the hills and ranges above Shahdol. This man was a joyful pastor-teacher who owned one set of clothes and one shawl for warmth in cold weather. He walked barefoot everywhere he went carrying the Good News as a humble messenger. As we walked into the hot, barren hills beyond the Jeep trails in the scorched landscape, we saw no water, no wells. The temperature in April was 110 degrees F and would reach 130 degrees by summer. There were no trees. The people lived in stick huts.

Hiking to one of the larger stick shelters that maybe held 14–15 people, angry neighbors threw rocks and curses at us. They knew nothing about us except that we were obviously not from there. We kept moving up the hillside to the meeting hut.

Many people began to gather and lined up to ask for healing as we read scriptures and prayed. Two local pastors interpreted and advised us to pray boldly for the impossible requests of these people who were sick and living in deep poverty. They had no clean water and the women and children had swollen or distended bellies from drinking dirty and contaminated water.

They begged for clean water and healing of the worms and parasites in their stomachs. When they handed us containers of muddy water, we were told to pray the power of God would cleanse it. We prayed as instructed. We did not speak the same language, but we understood the language of desperation. We had no purified water, filters, iodine tablets. God would have to act.

It was humbling to be surrounded by so many desperate people for hours in that hot and dry place. It can be physically and emotionally draining. On one occasion in Jesus' ministry, a woman touched his clothes, and he felt that power had gone out of him. I remembered that story in our crowd of people in the hut.

Toward the end of the line a woman stepped forward and spoke in a low, gravelly voice—"I have a demon." I didn't have much experience with evil spirits or demon possession, but I recognized it immediately. One time a few years earlier I had encountered the same voice in a person attending a Christian retreat in Texas. One of my spiritual mentors, J. T. Seamands, had taught me to simply confront such a spirit, command it to leave, and send it to Jesus to be dealt with by him. J. T. had grown up in India of missionary parents, returned there as a missionary with his wife after college, and knew the spiritual realm. We used his method.

The possessed woman stared at us before her eyes rolled completely back in her head, and she fell flat on her back. It was my turn to pray, and I invited our team to continue praying against the evil spirit in her body. She shook violently and then lay still for a long while as we continued praying for others. "Heal the sick, cast out demons." These deeds and the words that accompany them do rise to God. Prayers from a remote hillside.

Greater Joy in Healing

"These twelve disciples Jesus sent out with instructions . . . heal the sick, cleanse the lepers, cast out demons; freely you received, freely give."
—Matthew 10: 5–8 (ESV)

I really like California. Seriously. Every single time I visit. We were attending an annual spiritual retreat in the Summer of 2000. Camp Sierra is nestled in the beautiful western slope of the majestic Sierra Nevada Mountains northeast of Fresno. The week-long family camp, the Sierra Christian Ashram, always reached its highpoint with a Healing Service on the last night of worship.

The founder of the Christian Ashram Movement, Dr. E. Stanley Jones, believed so much in the healing power of God's Spirit that he made the Healing Service an essential element of the Ashram experience. He also immersed the Ashram in prayer—open heart prayers, prayer groups, the prayer vigil, overflowing prayers.

Ashram is a Sanskrit word meaning both "away from hard work" and "to the work of the soul." It can mean something like a forest or mountain retreat centered around a spiritual teacher; our center was the person of Jesus Christ. The Christian Ashram began at Sat Tal, India, in 1930, and Jones brought it to Michigan in 1940 where it grew into a movement of 70 Christian Ashrams in North America meeting every year.

The Healing Service always follows a New Testament story of one of the healings performed by Jesus. The Christian answer is a total answer to human need and so the physical body must be included. This includes the physical, mental, emotional, and spiritual dimensions of human beings. Our greatest healings in the Ashram are often not directly in the Healing Service, but indirectly through surrendering to God our wrong mental and spiritual attitudes and damaged emotions all during the week. When these go, healing can flow! "Heal the sick."

Sometimes, long after the Ashram camp, we receive letters from a person who received healing. "Freely you have received, freely give." I want to share one letter, with permission, that describes healing, a special note from Josie Garcia, a young woman from East Los Angeles.

> August 24, 2000
>
> "Dear Tom,
>
> Hello. I got my Ashram camp pictures back and thought maybe you'd like this one. It's such an amazing place, isn't it? I also wanted to thank you for your faith through prayer.
>
> Every year I go to the healing service thinking I'm fine, and every year I'm touched by the service. But this year was more powerful than ever. I've never felt the Holy Spirit as strongly as that night. Just thinking about it makes my heart full.
>
> You prayed for physical healing, and I received it. The pain in my stomach and the other symptoms of internal infections have stopped. You also prayed for my emotional and spiritual healing. I was so terrified of going back into the hospital, yet I've found greater joy in my spiritual healing than in my physical healing. I'm so thankful for God's work through you, Tom.
>
> My faith is renewed and I'm happier now than I ever remember being. After the Healing Service, I went for my hour alone in the prayer room. It was awesome and I prayed for things I didn't even realize I needed to pray about. I wrote over six pages in my prayer journal, and

> I only stopped because my replacement (for the next hour) came. It was an amazing healing for me, and I just wanted to share that with you. I keep you in my prayers.
>
> In His Holy Name,
>
> Josie Garcia

Those were Sierra mountainside prayers. Words and Deeds that rise as a memorial to God.

A Quick Change of Plans

"This is my body, which is given for you.
Do this in remembrance of me."
—Luke 22: 18–20 (ESV)

We were spending the Summer School Term of 1997 in Altea, Spain, overseeing 55 Baptist college students from eight universities, teaching our courses at this tourist town on the Costa del Sol. Altea is right on the Mediterranean coast where people from all over Europe vacation.

Spain is primarily Roman Catholic by religious affiliation with beautiful cathedrals and landmarks. The Spanish observe many religious festivals and traditions which were open, public events for all to see, including the Holy Eucharist which is exclusively for Catholics. One time I got in line to eat the bread and drink from the shared cup. Well, catholic does mean universal.

On June 25,1997, a Wednesday, I got up about 9:30 am in our dorm room at Lope de Vega School in Benidorm where some of our groups were being lodged that summer. We knew we would sleep late because our Spanish hosts insisted that we attend the Fires of St. John celebration in Alicante the night before. The Spaniards love the nightlife and their religious festivals. We delayed all Wednesday morning classes to the afternoon.

I walked that morning the mile or so to the Mediterranean for what I expected to be a nice run on the firm, wet sand of the beach. Our family of five had been attending worship most Sundays at the English Church, right on the beachfront at Benidorm. Without even thinking about it, my walk was taking me right past this storefront church. A retired pastor from England, Rev. Ray Whittle, served this church in Spain and another one in Zimbabwe. Brother Ray saw me first and waving to me said, "Brother Tom we're so glad you are coming to Wednesday Communion!" I said, "Thank-you," made a quick internal change of plans, and entered the small church. Brother Ray always began with Jesus. "If you don't begin with Jesus, you don't really begin."

Do this in remembrance of Jesus . . . until He returns.

1. *Do this* or *This do* is a command, an imperative. Holy Communion is more than a duty or a ritual—it is a celebration of Christ's presence by the bread and the wine. This sacrament—the Eucharist, Holy Communion, Lord's Supper—is observed monthly or quarterly in some churches but was practiced weekly in the early church. Observed infrequently, we Christians even tend to forget. It is an essential sacrament to the faith of a disciple, a pilgrim who celebrates Christ's presence with us.
2. *In remembrance.* It is more than remembering or calling the past to mind. We remember loved ones now absent. We look at vacation pictures of family and friends and recall the good times. But this is much deeper. We do not simply remember the Jesus who was, we experience the Jesus who is! He is present every time we break the bread and drink from the cup. (Perhaps that explains Christ's absence when we observe Communion infrequently.)
3. *Until He returns.* We are commanded to "Do this" now. But there will come a time when we will no longer have to break bread and drink the cup to know His presence. When He returns, we will know Him eternally and will dwell with Him. The Table will be necessary no longer! Unlike the pagans who speak of the end of the world, we have the promise of His

return. So, we begin by remembering. *Do this in remembrance of Me until I return.*

These words and this deed do rise as a memorial to God, every time!

Healing Physical and Spiritual Blindness

"The blind can see, the lame can walk, those who suffer from dreaded skin diseases are made clean, the deaf hear, the dead are brought back to life, and the Good News is preached to the poor."
—Matthew 11:5 (Good News Translation)

My daughter Savanah and I were traveling in Kenya for three weeks in 2001. The mission trip was designed with three different purposes in mind: (1) to serve the youth and local people in Butere, Western Kenya, near the border with Uganda; (2) to learn and observe the ministry of the Lighthouse for Christ Eye Clinic in Mombasa, Eastern Kenya, a development client of my consulting firm; and (3) to meet and visit with Church leaders in Nairobi.

Our itinerary included a layover and a day in London to see the sights of that great city. Fresh from watching the movie *The Parent Trap*, Savanah made a comprehensive list of "must see" places to fill that one day on our schedule. After sightseeing so much, we rested on our long flight to Nairobi. There we would transfer to a Kenya Airways flight to Kisumu in Kenya's western region.

The week we spent in youth and church ministry in that rural area was a real blessing to us, except for one health-related incident. We faithfully and daily took our malaria pills and were careful with food and water recommendations. The last day there, Savanah got a bad intestinal bug and was sick for several days on our drives and flights from Kisumu to Nairobi and on to Mombasa. I will spare you the details.

After the long journey to our rooms at the Lighthouse compound in Mombasa, Savanah was feeling better, and I shared my moments of worry and anxiety for her. (I had promised my wife that nothing bad would happen to our twelve-year-old daughter while in Kenya). I asked her if in the last two days she had been afraid. She answered promptly, "Dad, we are people of faith, not people of fear." That attitude could summarize our entire trip.

Mombasa is a city of 1.5 million people and predominantly Moslem by religious affiliation. The Lighthouse for Christ Eye Clinic is located near the Old Harbor on a major street, an accessible location for all our patients. We treat 40,000 patients every year without charge and today have additional services for pediatrics, an optical clinic, a private surgery clinic, and training facilities for doctors, staff, and pastors. In the heart of the city, one can hear the Muslim call to prayer five times daily.

Savanah and I met the missionaries, medical staff, and we volunteered in practical ways around the clinic. I was able to lead some training classes for pastors in the Bible School, and we visited a few of the 100 churches in this coastal area of Kenya. We were treated to some beach time on the coast of the Indian Ocean and a game safari at Tsavo National Park. Our week there equipped me to prepare a capital campaign for a new surgical operating theater and meet key leaders for that effort.

Our third week was spent at the Methodist Guest House (MGH) in Nairobi and was not planned out in our original schedule but was directed by God. "Man makes his plans; but God directs our steps." God opened doors there that I could only imagine. Board members from Kenya Methodist University in Meru "happened" to be meeting at the MGH on the same days. We met them and we met Bishop Lawi Imathiu of the British Methodist Church in Kenya. Open Door #1.

The KMU board mentioned a new charitable foundation in the States that made grants to African nonprofits. I contacted the Foundation as soon as we returned home and we soon received a $40,000 gift for our Lighthouse Capital Campaign. Open Door #2.

The next Spring the KMU Board met in Macon, Georgia, and we developed our relationship with Bishop Imathiu even deeper. He was a visionary leader who became the Kenyan Bishop, founded and built Kenya Methodist University, and imagined the Methodist Guest House into reality. Open Door #3.

Bishop Imathiu was a humble leader who always reminded all of us that "we stand on the shoulders of those who came before us." He grew up in a large family and never had a pair of shoes until he was an adult. He gives credit to the young British missionaries who came to Kenya more than 150 years before, knowing that with no roads nor hospitals that they would likely never return home to the UK. *The Good News is preached to the poor.* (The rich don't think they need it!)

The Kenyan pastors in Butere, the medical doctors, staff, and volunteers in Mombasa, and the many teachers, professors, and employees of the Methodist institutions in Nairobi and Meru perform deeds and use good words every day that are "Words and Deeds that rise as a Memorial to God." They rise and they pile-up and they accumulate as they come to God's attention.

That's Good News!

A Heart for Missions

"Go into all the world and proclaim the Good News to the whole creation." —Mark 16:15 (ESV)

Jesus was sent to Earth to fulfill a mission. Full-time Christian missions is a calling of God, a sending ministry. Some climbing companions of Jesus are the "sent ones," set apart by God to go to the nations and tribes and live among them. We know many such families and have supported some whom we have come to know and love. My wife and I weren't called to be full-time missionaries.

However, in the priesthood of believers, we are all missionaries in our neighborhoods, communities, cities, and towns. You have been given *a heart for missions.* I have done short-term missions in numerous countries. Our adult children have spent longer-term missions in Thailand, China, Honduras, and Ireland, as well as in the United States. Our daughter Mallary and her two sons, Pilgrim and Tasker, do summer mission trips in Montana. The boys are mountaineers and missionaries. *Trust God when doors open.*

God opened doors for me in Mexico, Honduras, Guatemala, and Costa Rica for short-term work projects, medical missions, pastor training events, and staff retreats. God will match your gifts and talents with the needs of people in other places. Your responsibility is to be F.I.T.—Faithful, Intentional, and Teachable. *Inside of every grace that God gives to a person hides a mission.*

Doors began to open for missions when I taught economics at Christian colleges and universities. Our spring break trips took us into Mexico numerous times. I planned the trips and kept the expenses low. Growing up I had relatives living in El Paso and I knew some full-time missionaries there. My commitment in those days was primarily cross-cultural experiences for my students. I always took with us several students who were fluent in Spanish.

In 2003 we took some seminary students to Costa Rica and did several work projects at churches—painting, simple carpentry, and Sunday worship. We took some time for recreation—zip lining, river rafting, and outdoor sports with kids. This trip was organized by a good friend who had connections with a Methodist Bishop there and all I had to do was say "Yes, I'll go." *Here I am, send me!*

This same friend re-connected me a mutual friend from our campus ministry days at Texas Tech University who was in full-time missions in Guatemala. I made the first trip alone to Guatemala City to attend their mission board meeting and meet the staff and volunteers of their children's home and K-12 school. I did some consulting with their leaders in strategy and fund development. I returned the next year to lead their annual missionary retreat in Antigua.

For a remarkable mission to Honduras in 2010, I was simply in the right place at the right time when God opened a door at the church my parents attended. My wife and I attended the informational meeting and signed up. This adventure combined work projects at an orphanage with a medical team serving the physical needs of people there. My wife had travelled to many countries in the world as a member of a touring Girls Choir, but she had never joined us on a mission trip. *The Honduran children stole her heart. She was hooked!*

Christian missions take many approaches to proclaiming the Good News AND they are all about building relationships across cultures. *Christianity is not a set of rules to follow but a relationship with Christ and our neighbors everywhere.*

Those relationships are built on a practice of prayer as outlined in this book: living close to God, letting your words and deeds rise to God, and lingering longer on prayer mountain with God. Desire produces discipline. The desire for God produces the disciplines of living, letting, and lingering.

My spiritual disciplines have been discovered in running, climbing, and exploring. *"They will run and not grow weary, walk and not be faint-hearted."* (Isaiah 40:31—one of my life verses) Perhaps you will find your disciplines in gardening, birdwatching, or dog training. Probably, in an avocation, I don't know. Possibly, outside in nature, I don't know. I encourage you to discover your own prayer practices.

Let's turn now to the lessons on prayer and the parallels from mountaineering, even as you discover your disciplines from your practice of daily praying. *For we do not know what to pray for as we ought, but the Spirit of God intercedes for us.* (Rom 8:26 ESV) Your prayer practices will be your *sheath* in abrasive times and durability in resistance.

THE THIRD STRAND

Prayer Practices for Hearing God

Prayer Practices for Hearing God

Prayer is not a passive discipline. Many people, both religious and non-religious, view prayer as a quiet, contemplative non-activity. Where the customs of prayer—time of day, invocation, mealtime, bedtime, benediction—are observed, we are supposed to close our eyes, bow our heads, and allow someone else to do the praying. We are taught to think prayer is passive.

It is even of some comfort to us that certain people have cloistered themselves and taken up the vocation of prayer, surrendering as well to a simpler way of life. They pray for the world. But this kind of prayer is not passive either. We permit ourselves to think so.

Prayer is an *active* discipline. It is a call to active duty. God is calling us to enter the spiritual battle, to wrestle and struggle, to move, to climb. "When Jesus saw his ministry drawing huge crowds, he climbed a hillside. Those who were apprenticed to Him, the committed, climbed with Him. Arriving a quiet place, He sat down and taught His climbing companions." (Matt 5:1–2 MSG)

Jesus reminds us that the discipline of prayer results in action. *In prayer there is a connection between what God does and what you do. You can't get forgiveness from God, for instance, without also forgiving others. (Matt 6: 14–15 MSG)*

Prayer customs are just symbols. The inner reality is a radical dependence upon God. This is the true posture of prayer. While there are times to "be still and know that I am God," Jesus expects disciples to be his climbing companions. We are marching upward, passing through the wilderness, and climbing summits! We must know God in our active pursuits, our abrasions producing durability. *God is sheath-like, daily discipline being your sheath.*

On the bedroom wall of a mountain retreat in Northern India near the great Himalayas, a mighty prayer warrior encouraged himself with these framed words: *Be vigilant, praying at all times, to come safely through all that lies ahead of you and stand before the Son of Man.*

The Yoido Full Gospel Church in Seoul, South Korea, has a retreat area called Prayer Mountain dedicated to prayer. Thousands and thousands of people go there daily to get their needs met and to practice fasting and praying. This is probably the most prayer-concentrated place on Earth.

We designed and implemented a series of weekend prayer events that we called *Climbing Prayer Mountain (CPM).* God was then and is now calling His followers to active praying. We took the active practice of hiking and mountain climbing and identified ten parallels that we applied to our prayer lives. Together, as a sacred fellowship, we sought God's vision and mission for the new year.

As climbing companions of Jesus, let us pursue an active posture and practice of prayer. *He who forms the mountains, creates the wind, and reveals His thoughts to mankind; He who turns dawn to darkness, and treads the high places of the Earth—the LORD God Almighty is His Name. —Amos 4:13 (NASB)*

Consider these ten parallels and principles for your practice of prayer. These practices keep us going to the mountainside with God and going on mission, as God reveals his thoughts to us.

The Mountain is Life and Life is the Mountain

Climbing mountains is always challenging, hiking the initial approach or bouldering the final summit push. *Always.* Read this excerpt that I saw recently about a hike over the Alborz Mountains to the Caspian Sea: *To reach the base of Alamut rock was an easy 20-minute walk, but the steep and scrambling climb up the mountain wedge left us sweaty and winded . . . I stopped to rest many times along the way . . . Up top was a narrow ridge about 400 yards long, with near-vertical cliffs falling off on all sides.*[4]

It is typical in approaching a tall mountain that there are valleys to ascend, alpine meadows with overgrown sedges and grasses to traverse, and often swollen streams and rivers to cross. These are good days though the mountain itself lies far ahead. Rising above the timberline, rocky ridges appear with miles of switchbacks leading upward to a connecting or summit ridge.

The air is thinner as you ascend rockslides and snowfields. *Is the mountain only interested in obstacles to my progress?* Some climbing days we encounter bottomless blue crevasses and blinding white avalanches. *Where is the trail? Why am I always short of breath?* We encounter one false summit after another.

4. Christiane Bird, *Neither East nor West: One Woman's Journey Through the Islamic Republic of Iran*. New York: Pocket, 2001, page 25.

Does this resemble life? Is the challenge similar? Is the parallel relevant? Life is a continual challenge, rising and falling and rising again. Life's valleys and detours can take extra time to pass through, hope almost flickering out. Life can seem like a long expedition on foot, progressing slowly the routes and maps we think are accurate. Discouragement is the companion of even the most experienced trekker and hiker. Ask an older climber about the treacherous terrain and vertical cliffs ahead. *Does it ever get easier? No.*

We all have mountains in life. What "mountain" are you facing? Which do you need more: Core strength, Core Stretch, Sheath? Prayer is the Rope. It is a symbol, a reminder. Perhaps you've seen pictures of the prayer flags at Everest Base Camp, blessing the surrounding area, elevation 17,600 feet. A symbol. They are used to promote peace, strength, and wisdom in that high-altitude environment. The prayer rope is a symbol.

Stay roped to Jesus and continue climbing. Listen to God on the mountain.

> *I lift my eyes up to the mountains. Where does my help come from? My help comes from the Lord, who made heaven and earth and the mountains.—Psalm 121*

Prayer Is the Inner Strength

Living the vertical life and moving forward requires desire and discipline. *Desire produces discipline and desire is born in the heart.* Christ in my heart creates a conversation, a prayer. This intimate conversation goes beyond saying prayers or tossing a desperate "Hail Mary" passing prayer. Life, like the mountain, demands more of our *strength and stretch.* Faith and risk are courage-words, emerging from the same root word. Faith, meaning trust, is an action-oriented verb.

The climbing companion of Jesus, the active Christ-follower, is no timid soul content with safe and familiar paths:

The elements of walking are properly mastered on well-marked, well-manicured trails; indeed, the majority of hikers, to minimize danger and nastiness, choose never to stray from the comparative friendliness of turnpike terrain. Others, though are called so loud and clear by wilderness, are compelled so urgently by an inner force stronger than reason that they climb above the trails into brush, up rocks and snows to tall summits.

Believers are called loud and clear to climb higher, further up and further in. The compelling voice of the Indwelling Christ calls us to prayer mountain. Pray by the clock until you can pray by the heart. Develop the *strength and stretch* of the core person. *Your inner stances are greater than your circumstances when you pray.* Go out to face the mountain with inner strength and perspective.

> *"Be strong and take heart, all you who hope in the Lord."*
> *—Psalm 31*

An Individual and Team Effort

Hikers and climbers, like those who practice regular prayer, are drawn to the hills and mountains, wild places. These places draw us into a sense of personal retreat, toward a mystery not yet seen. Some seek companionship on their beginner's hikes while others venture out alone. Individuals who hike and climb are rewarded with a feeling of accomplishment. "I did it!" I grow; I improve.

Something or Someone bigger than ourselves compels us to pray. We find that it is in our nature to pray. We are made for talks with God. We cry out to the heavens with God-designed emotions. Anyone can be taught prayer principles and learn to pray effectively. *But God draws us to prayer.* God has placed the desire within human nature. *Like the deer pants for the water, so we thirst for God.*

Initially, prayer is an individual pursuit, a personal and private relationship with Abba, Father. It matures into *team* effort. Personal prayer naturally leads to prayer with and for others. Group prayer can be intimidating at first and properly led does not require every person to pray out loud. In climbing language, the team is roped together for *strength and stretch.* We pray for ourselves and the needs of others. Friends pray for us. It is the way we climb the toughest mountains of life. *A prayer warrior is a person dedicated to prayer, praying for and with others.*

> *"As the deer pants for streams of water, so I long for you, O God."*—Psalm 42:1

Base Camp is the Prayer Closet

Base Camp on the mountain is a place of provision. It is the place that climbers leave from and return to. It is a place of relative safety and acclimatization for the higher camps. We descend the mountain returning to base camp to rest, recover, and re-supply. On the world's highest mountain, Mt. Everest (29,035 feet), South Base Camp in Nepal is located along the left edge of Khumbu Glacier just below Khumbu Icefall at an elevation of 17,600 feet. North Base Camp in Tibet sits at 16,900 feet. Teams bring many loads of provisions to Base Camp before carrying supplies to higher camps.

The prayer closet (Matthew 6:6) is the prayer warrior's base camp. It is a place of spiritual provision and solace. The author believes that the hillside or mountainside is the example that Jesus practiced and taught for living close to God. It is a place we can depart from and return to each day. We dare not enter the day without gaining inner *strength and stretch* first. Prayer must be a fixture on the mountain of our life.

In an even broader sense, Base Camp is also a place where dreams are forged, where connections are formed, and where histories are framed (written). On a personal note, Base Camp is where my dream was *forged*: climb the highest mountain in all fifty states and travel on all seven continents. Base Camp is where I *formed* spiritual friends and climbing companions. Base Camp is where I *framed* my history and legacy. I need a Base Camp.

What is your dream? Who are your companions? What will be your legacy?

> "I have set you an example that you should do as I have done for you."—John 13:15
>
> "*Be still, and know that I am God.*"—Psalm 46:10

Obstacles and Interruptions

Like life itself, mountains are known for being unpredictable, shifting and changing. Unexpected snowstorms, swollen streams and rivers, blue sky lightning, wild animal encounters, heavy snow and avalanches, mountaineering carries these risks in strenuous conditions. Climbing involves risk management due to surprises and unplanned obstacles. Rewards lie on the other side.

Prayer can be uplifting, comforting, and fulfilling on many occasions. And it comes with its own list of obstacles, detours, and interruptions:

- Wandering thoughts
- False guilt
- Impure thoughts
- Vengeful thoughts
- Interruptions
- Asking for the wrong things
- Failure to ask
- Lack of commitment or discipline
- Sin and unbelief
- Unforgiving spirit
- Doubt and fear
- Powers and principalities

Expect the unexpected. Pray through the obstacles. Use the interruptions. *If you are interrupted, let the interruption be an interpretation.* Don't let the interruption keep you distracted from your prayer time. The habit of daily prayer on the mountainside will be richer by overcoming obstacles and interruptions. *Prayer is an action step, and it is an internal attitude. Make your interruptions a prayer. The universe is an open universe.*

> "If I had been cozy with evil, the Lord would never have listened. But he most surely *did* listen."—Psalm 66:18

Carrying Loads Higher

The mountain climber carries her own provisions and survival gear for the team to higher camps. Backpacks can weigh 60–70 pounds and big mountains like Denali require pulling a sled of supplies as well. On some mountains, porters or sherpas are hired to carry equipment and food, setting up higher camps for the climbers. A young and very fit climber friend of mine just returned from Denali. The weather kept them from the summit. He told me the climb was the toughest one that he had ever done.

Persistent prayer is like that. We carry our own heavy loads and the burdens of others. Prayer certainly involves listening to God and making petitions of God. But it also includes intercession—going to God in prayer for other people. *This is tough work.*

Intercessory prayer (carrying burdens) has three defining characteristics:

1. Putting the full weight of these burdens on God while he cleanses your heart.
2. Waiting expectantly to hear the response of Jesus.
3. Being directed by the Holy Spirit gives you guidance on how to pray and how to listen and how to go.

Prayers for your burdens and prayer for others is a privilege given to mature Christ followers as this hymn from the 1940s says:

> *Are we weak and heavy-laden, cumbered with a load of care? Precious Savior, still our refuge, Take it to the Lord in prayer. What a privilege it is to carry, Everything to God in prayer.*

I have a large manila folder in my file cabinet which contains the prayer requests of hundreds of people. For more than 40 years I have been teaching prayer to individuals and groups. We practice the habit of praying together and I often record the prayers in this now two-inch thick folder. It is a journal of God's faithfulness when His people pray in humility and surrender to His will. The prayers of a person living right with God is something powerful to be reckoned with. (James 5:16)

> *"If your heart is broken, you'll find God right there; if you're kicked in the gut, he'll help you catch your breath."*
> —Psalm 34:18 (MSG)

Acclimate to the Altitude

Climbers need to be aware of sudden changes in altitude from sea level on the approach to elevations above 14,000 feet at base camp. Symptoms of altitude sickness like headache, nausea, or hypothermia can come on suddenly and can affect even people accustomed to climbing. If they do, the best and most effective treatment is getting back down the mountain to lower elevations.

Praying has a parallel. I call it "prayer exposure." Saying prayers before meals or bedtimes is good training for children but it doesn't attract much attention in the higher spiritual realms. Praying constantly for an hour or more does. Like exposure to altitude, the spiritual atmosphere is thinner in the heights. Here are a few quotes from some *giants of the Christian faith:*

The realm of God is dangerous. You must enter it and not just seek information about it.[5]

Occasional joggers do not suddenly enter an Olympic marathon. They prepare and train themselves over a period of time. So should we.[6]

For our struggle is not against flesh and blood, but against the rulers, against the powers, against the world forces of this

5. Peterson, Eugene. *Working The Angles: The Shape of Pastoral Integrity.* Grand Rapids: Eerdman's, 1989, page 31.

6. Foster, Richard. *Celebration of Discipline.* New York: Harper and Row, 1978, page 31.

darkness, against the spiritual forces of wickedness in the heavenly places. (St. Paul—Ephesians 6:12)

> "I waited and waited and waited for God. At last, he looked; finally, he listened."—Psalm 40:1–4

Rise Early to Summit

Due to climbing conditions and weather factors on mountains, a summit attempt usually begins in the early morning hours. It is common to depart for the summit around 2:00 or 3:00 a.m. to reach the top by midday and then get down off the mountain. Morning people or not, climbers rise early. On an ascent of Mt. Kenya, we were up before midnight and climbing in a snowstorm to ascend at the right time to see the sun rise over Africa.

As we have seen in the FIRST STRAND, living close to God often means rising early. *And in the early morning, He arose and went out and departed to a lonely place and was praying there.* Jesus who is our teacher and example, went out to pray long before it was daylight. Even today his climbing companions do the same.

I know that some people are morning people and others are night owls. I know that good folks work night shifts and that work schedules vary. Some faithful prayer warriors carve out prayer at other times of day. We are encouraged to *pray without ceasing.*

Climbers don't climb a big mountain every day. When they do, they start early on summit day. Prayer warriors don't face big challenges every day. When they do, they rise early and occasionally pray all night long. C.S. Spurgeon reflecting on the words of Martin Luther said, "Luther thought that the more he had to do, the more he must pray, or else he could not get through it. This is a blessed kind of logic." *You cannot afford to not pray.*

"God's there, listening for all who pray, for all who pray and mean it."—Psalm 145:18

A Radiant Face

Mountain climbers may have more than a summit sunburn; it may be the radiant glow of accomplishment on their faces. Weariness or fatigue is often visible back at camp after a long day but beneath that the climber radiates something of his mountain-top experience. *Climbing is hard, and victories don't come easily.*

"Moses did not know that the skin of his face shown because of his speaking with God." (Exodus 34:29) Like Moses coming down from Mt. Sinai and the presence of God, prayer warriors are often unaware of their inner light and facial countenance. As I recall the names and faces of my prayer mentors—Jordan, Eloise, Joe, Gail, Donna, Roberta, Terry, J.T., Bill, Gordon—they glowed because they lived close to God. It showed on their faces.

Like climbing high mountains and almost touching the sun, praying regularly puts a glow on your face. You have spent time alone with the Lord God. *The radiance of their faces meant they spent daily time with God.* Perhaps you remember meeting, or you personally knew one of these prayer warriors who live close to God.

> *"Those who look to God are radiant; their faces are never covered with shame."*—Psalm 34:5

Supernatural Silence

Peter Matthiessen, author of *The Snow Leopard*, writes this beautiful insight about silence high on the mountains:

> *"Snow mountains, more than sea or sky, serve as a mirror to one's own true being, utterly still, utterly clear, a void, an Emptiness without life or sound that carries in Itself all life, all sound."*[7]

I have known these snow mountains. My experience of them was even more profound in Antarctica, the white continent. The vast white wilderness there exudes a silence that is only broken at times along the coast by waves crashing and glaciers calving into the sea. Sara Wheeler, author of *Terra Incognita*, says of Antarctica, "It was like seeing the earth for the very first time, and I felt less homeless there than I had ever felt anywhere."

Morning prayers are often called "morning quiet time" and "alone time with God." We hear God better in silence and quiet places. The mountain summits and wilderness places of the world have this silence in common. So do the times of mountainside prayer. Praying opens doors. We are ushered into the presence of God. His silence is His answer, our answer. We live close to God.

> *"Step out of the traffic! Take a long, loving look at your High God, above everything."*—Psalm 46:10 (MSG)

7. Peter Matthiessen, *The Snow Leopard*. New York: Penguin Random House, 2008, page 115.

THE FOURTH STRAND

Climbing Prayer Mountain

Pray or Lose Heart

Jesus put the alternatives this way: Men and women should always pray, and not faint. It is Pray OR Faint—literally! Those who pray do not faint, and those who faint do not pray.

You can become ALIVE to your fingertips:

- Every cell in your body alert, active, creative.
- You can enjoy health and have all you need.
- You can have life and life more abundantly.

PROVIDED YOU PRAY . . . Otherwise, you faint—you lose heart, you resign, you give up.

Jesus prayed (prayer is the battle) and went calmly and confidently to the Cross. The victory was won at Gethsemane. His disciples were calm in the Garden and fell apart in the heat!

PRAY OR FAINT . . .

ALIGNING OUR PRAYING WITH THE LIFE OF GOD

God wants, longs for, desires, to perform this alignment in our lives. We see this surrender throughout scripture.

> *For the eyes of the LORD are on the righteous and His ears are attentive to their prayer, but the face of the LORD is against those who do evil.*—1 Peter 3:12

But you, dear friends, build yourselves up in your most holy faith and pray in the Holy Spirit.—Jude 1:20

We do not know what we ought to pray for, but the Holy Spirit himself intercedes for us with groans (Utterances) that words cannot express. And He who searches our hearts knows the mind of the Spirit, because the Spirit intercedes for the saints (climbing companions) in accordance with God's will.—Rom 8:26

A Fixed Line for Anchored Prayer

In mountain climbing a fixed line is a rope that is anchored and left in place on the route. I like the imagery for intentional, anchored prayer.

1. Fix your daily time of prayer.
2. State what you long for in your prayer time.
3. Decide to make each prayer a Christlike one.
4. Write down your prayer requests.
5. Glorify God by stilling your mind.
6. Converse with God by first listening, then speaking.
7. Recall God's promises and make your promise to God.
8. Love your enemies and forgive your critics.
9. Thank God in advance for His answers, His way.
10. Release each prayer to rise to God's throne.

Simple Helps for a Richer Prayer Life

Five Elements of Prayer:

1. Worship and Adoration of God
2. Thanksgiving
3. Confession
4. Petition
5. Intercession

A Simple Prayer Pattern:

Adoration

Confession

Thanksgiving

Supplication

Using this ACTS acronym, begin your by praising and expressing love for God. Confess your sins to Him. Thank Him for His mercy and forgiveness toward you. Bring to Him your personal concerns and requests for others. Each of the four parts may only be one sentence. Be honest with God.

Action Verbs for Prayer:

Persisting . . . Keep asking, seeking, knocking Matthew 7

Receiving . . . As many as received Him Matthew 10

Asking . . . Whatever you ask for Matthew 21

Yielding . . . Thy will be done Matthew 26

Expecting . . . Pray then like this Matthew 6

Releasing . . . The Father rewards in secret Matthew 6

Use this **PRAYER** acronym and discern each of the six elements in your praying. Always end by *releasing* your requests and prayers to God.

FINISHING WELL

Prayer opens the door to exorbitant grace! God's grace is unbounded! God is willing to open the gates and pour out his grace upon us. Grace is God's unmerited favor. God pours out his favor even though we don't deserve it, can't earn it, are reluctant to accept it. God loves. Prayer is *our* response to *his* ability, the ability to rain down mercy on us. Walking in prayer opens wide the doors and windows of Heaven!

It is like this. I am a ten-year-old boy. I have been playing outside as usual. I walk inside the house to my mother's kitchen. I was unaware of it, but she baked an angel food cake and had just finished spreading the chocolate icing on the cake. (I love chocolate icing more than cake!) She asks me, "Tombo, do you want the rest of the chocolate icing in the bowl?" "Sure Mom!" I didn't earn it. I didn't deserve it. I just walked through the door. And then I went back outside.

Prayer opens the door to exorbitant grace!

Live close to God. Go in the grace of God. Let your words and deeds rise. Keep climbing prayer mountain. Pray or Lose Heart.

Mountainside Playlist

"A Dream Remembers"—John Fluker

"Be Thou My Vision"—David Nevue

"Church of Trees"—Liz Story

"Come Home"—Mike Howe

"Down Along the Lines of Joy"—Mark Kroos

"Early Morning Range"—George Winston

"Eternal"—David Tolk

"Gratitude"—Liz Story

"Gospel"—Michael Hedges

"Hallowed Fire"—Mairead Nesbitt

"Heaven's Light"—David Tolk

"Hymn"—Liz Story

"Jordan's Shore"—Doug Smith

"Living with Hope"—Helen Jane Long

"Long Awaited Love"—Thad Fiscella

"My Shepherd Will Supply My Need"—Doug Smith

"Near the Cross"—Fernando Ortega

"Nighttime in the Chapel"—Will Ackerman

"Once I Prayed"—Phil Keaggy

"Peace March"—Bruce Cockburn

"Prayer"—Phil Keaggy

"Reconciliation"—Liz Story

"Sorrow Floats"—Ben Woolman

"The Eye of God"—Stephen Bennett

"The Opening of Doors"—Will Ackerman

"Those Who Wait"—Tommy Emmanuel

"To The Summit"—David Tolk

www.ingramcontent.com/pod-product-compliance
Lightning Source LLC
LaVergne TN
LVHW020654100826
845148LV00012B/2478